Signs and Wonders Follow You

Also by Joseph Achanya

Signs and Wonders Follow You

Shaking Your Generation

Signs and Wonders Follow You

Living a Life of Miracles Daily

Joseph Achanya

Without limiting the rights under copyright(s) reserved below, no part of this publication may be reproduced, stored in or introduced into a retrieval system, or transmitted in any form or by any means (electronic, mechanical, photocopying, recording, or otherwise) without the prior permission of the publisher and the copyright owner.

The content of this book is provided "AS IS." The publisher and the author make no guarantees or warranties as to the accuracy, adequacy or completeness of or results to be obtained from using the content of this book, including any information that can be accessed through hyperlinks or otherwise, and expressly disclaim any warranty expressed or implied, including but not limited to implied warranties of merchantability or fitness for a particular purpose. This limitation of liability shall apply to any claim or cause whatsoever, whether such claim or cause arises in contract, tort, or otherwise. In short, you, the reader, are responsible for your choices and the results they bring.

The scanning, uploading, and distributing of this book via the internet or any other means without the permission of the publisher and copyright owner is illegal and punishable by law. Please purchase only authorized copies, and do not participate in or encourage piracy of copyrighted materials. Your support of the author's rights is appreciated.

Copyright © 2024 by Joseph Achanya. All rights reserved.

Released November 2024
ISBN: 978-1-64457-663-2

Rise UP Publications
www.riseUPpublications.com

Unless otherwise noted, all Scriptures are from the KING JAMES VERSION, public domain.

Scripture quotations marked (NLT) are taken from the Holy Bible, New Living Translation, copyright ©1996, 2004, 2015 by Tyndale House Foundation. Used by permission of Tyndale House Publishers, Carol Stream, Illinois 60188. All rights reserved.

Scripture quotations marked (NIV) are taken from THE HOLY BIBLE, NEW INTERNATIONAL VERSION®. Copyright© 1973, 1978, 1984, 2011 by Biblica, Inc.™. Used by permission of Zondervan

Scripture quotations marked (NRSV) are taken from the New Revised Standard Version Bible, copyright © 1989 the Division of Christian Education of the National Council of the Churches of Christ in the United States of America. Used by permission. All rights reserved.

To the life and ministry of Dr. T.L. Osborn who remains the greatest inspiration for my miracle ministry.

Contents

Introduction	11
Chapter 1 *Healing is God's Idea*	15
Chapter 2 *This Same Jesus!*	23
Chapter 3 *The Origin of Sickness and Disease*	29
Chapter 4 *Creative Miracles*	37
Chapter 5 *You Can Be Sure*	45
Chapter 6 *The Realities Of Redemption*	51
Chapter 7 *Act Accordingly*	61
Chapter 8 *Church Of Healing*	69
Chapter 9 *According To My Gospel*	73
Chapter 10 *Cessationism Debunked With Seven Questions*	79
Chapter 11 *Healing Scriptures*	91
Chapter 12 *Healing Prayer*	109
Shaking Your Generation	113
About the Author	115

Introduction

And these signs shall follow them that believe...

— Mark 16:17

These were some of Jesus' last words, a promise to anyone who believes in Him: signs and wonders shall follow you. They will follow you to every meeting, every service, and every city, whether you are on the platform or not, whether you are asleep or awake, whether you feel anointed or not.

In Acts 3, Peter prayed for the man who was lame from birth at the Beautiful Gate, commanding him to rise up and walk. This miracle astonished the rulers.

> *Saying, What shall we do to these men? for that indeed a notable miracle hath been done by them is manifest to all them that dwell in Jerusalem; and we cannot deny it.*
>
> — Acts 4:16

Introduction

To them, that was a notable miracle. It marveled the entire synagogue. But to Peter, miracles were a daily occurrence. He was surprised that they were surprised.

> *Peter saw his opportunity and addressed the crowd. "People of Israel," he said, "what is so surprising about this? And why stare at us as though we had made this man walk by our own power or godliness?"*

> — Acts 3:12 (NLT)

We shouldn't be surprised when a miracle happens; we should be surprised when a miracle doesn't happen. Think of it this way: imagine a judge visiting a prison and seeing a criminal he has sentenced. Amazed, the judge asks, "Why are you here?" The criminal replies, "You sentenced me to 10 years in prison." Then, the judge says, "Wow! I didn't think they would put you in prison. I was not feeling well when I made the sentence." It doesn't matter how the judge feels; once he hits the gavel, his words become a decree, and he shouldn't be shocked at the outcome!

Jesus' earthly ministry was full of signs and wonders. Every chapter in the Gospels contains a sign and a wonder. So did the early church. In fact, every chapter in the Book of Acts had a supernatural experience. That's our model: signs and wonders daily. When the Lord called me into the ministry, He said, "Your ministry must be nothing short of the supernatural!" That is God's expectation for every believer.

In this book, I communicate everything I know concerning signs, wonders, and miracles. You will discover how to live a life experiencing miracles everywhere you go. This book will

Introduction

be a tool in the hands of believers, Bible school students, preachers, and gospel workers to help them exalt Jesus daily.

Chapter One

Healing is God's Idea

First Mention of Healing in the Bible

I want to start by looking at the first time divine healing was mentioned in the Bible. You can discover great truths by examining the passages where the subject is first mentioned. Healing is first found in Genesis chapter 20.

To summarize the story, Abraham was married to Sarah, a very attractive woman. Fearing that someone might harm him to take his wife, Abraham told Sarah to lie and say that she was his sister. King Abimelech sent for Sarah and had her brought to his palace. However, God came to the king at night in a dream and told him he was a dead man if he didn't return Sarah because she was married.

> *Now therefore restore the man his wife; for he is a prophet, and he shall pray for thee, and thou shalt live: and if thou restore her not, know thou that thou shalt surely die, thou, and all that are thine.*
>
> — Genesis 20:7

King Abimelech returned Sarah immediately with money and land as compensation.

> *So Abraham prayed unto God: and God healed Abimelech, and his wife, and his maidservants; and they bare children. For the Lord had fast closed up all the wombs of the house of Abimelech, because of Sarah Abraham's wife.*
>
> — Genesis 20:17-18

Prayer for Healing Was God's Idea

From that story, we see that it wasn't Abimelech's or Abraham's idea to pray for healing; it was God's idea. God was the one who said to go to Abraham because he is a prophet, and he will pray for you, and you will live! That changes the narrative. It means we are not the ones trying to beg or convince God to do a miracle. It was His idea, His intention. Abraham prayed, and God healed. That's how it works today: we pray, and God heals. God is the Healer, and His passion is healing.

> *...They shall lay hands on the sick, and they shall recover.*
>
> — Mark 16:18

Healing is still God's idea. The great commission was God's idea. People go on long, extended fasts to "get God interested in the sick." But long before you were born, God was already interested in healing.

It was God's idea to perform signs and wonders in Egypt.

Signs and Wonders Follow You

> *"So I will raise my hand and strike the Egyptians, performing all kinds of miracles among them. Then at last he will let you go."*
>
> — Exodus 3:20 (NLT)

It was God's idea to bring the Israelites out of Egypt without sickness.

> *He brought them forth also with silver and gold: and there was not one feeble person among their tribes.*
>
> — Psalm 105:37

It was God's idea to send His Son, Jesus. He could have sent Jesus solely to die for our sins, but He also took away our sicknesses and diseases.

> *Who his own self bare our sins in his own body on the tree, that we, being dead to sins, should live unto righteousness: by whose stripes ye were healed.*
>
> — 1 Peter 2:24

It was God's idea to give His disciples power and authority over sickness and diseases.

> *Then he called his twelve disciples together, and gave them power and authority over all devils, and to cure diseases.*
>
> — Luke 9:1

Joseph Achanya

Jehovah Rapha

...for I am the Lord that healeth thee.

— Exodus 15:26

There are many names for God. Jehovah Jireh, which means "The Lord will provide," was the name Abraham called God when He provided the ram to be sacrificed in place of Isaac. The name Jehovah Nissi, which means "The Lord our Banner," was the name Moses gave to God when the Lord gave the Israelites victory over the Amalekites. These are just two of the many examples of men who had a revelation of God and gave Him a name.

But what is different about the name Jehovah Rapha, which means "The Lord our Healer"? The difference is that no man called God a healer; He called Himself the Healer. He gave Himself the name! He wants to be known by that name! He is the Healer of all nations.

We do not fast and pray to convince God or get Him interested in the sick; God planned it from the beginning. Jesus paid for it, and the Holy Spirit distributes it. God is who He says He is—Jehovah Rapha. God will do what He promised to do. When I stand on the platform before a multitude of people who are in pain, sick, and suffering, my confidence is in the fact that I know God is more willing to do a miracle than I want Him to do a miracle. God is not going to put me to shame; rather, Jesus will be glorified! This is not man convincing God; this is God's passion.

God introduced Himself in the Bible as a healer. He is called Jehovah Rapha. If you do not believe that, then you do not believe in the Bible. If you do not believe in healing, then you do not believe in the Bible.

I heard the story of a man who had a Bible, and it was a very skinny Bible because he had torn out many pages. What was left was a very tiny portion of the Bible. Someone saw him and asked him what had happened to his Bible. He said, "Oh, we have a very great pastor. He is a theologian, and every time my pastor taught and would say a particular part of the Bible was not for today, I would tear that part out. When he said healing is not for today, I tore that part out. Whatever he said wasn't for today or for me, I just tore it out. There is no point in keeping it there. This is what is left of the Bible."

You can't take healing out of the Bible. If you remove healing and the power of God from the Bible, the only thing that will remain would be the two covers of the Bible, because from Genesis to Revelation, we see a God who is a healer. A healing God is depicted in the Old Testament, a healing Jesus in the Gospels, and a healing church in the New Testament. The Bible is a book demonstrating the power of God.

There is nothing absolutely mysterious about healing. God is big, and your disease is small. God made the heavens, the sea, and the fishes. What can He not do? It is very simple. Do you think the God who made the heavens and this earth can't heal? Our God is a big God. He is bigger than the sea; He is wider than the oceans; He is taller than the mountains; our God is very big!

One day, I made a phone call and found out that the person on the other end could not hear me. What did I do? I took the phone to the mall. When you go to the mall, you find people who fix phones in the middle of the mall. I went and gave the phone to them, and they couldn't fix it. They said that I had to take it back to Apple because it was an iPhone. At that instant, I said to myself, "That's healing." Apple made the phone, and when something went wrong with it, I took it to the phone doctors. When the phone doctors couldn't fix it, they recommended that I return it to the manufacturer.

God made you. He made your body, your eyes, your legs, brain, lungs, and heart. When something goes wrong, we take it to the doctors, and the doctors do the best they can. When they find out there is nothing else they can do, they have to send you back to the manufacturer. That is healing. Healing is taking your body back to the one who made you and saying, "God, You can fix me. You made my eyes, You made my legs, and You can fix it." There is nothing mysterious about that.

That is what makes Him God. He is the God who does not change. He is the Lord who heals and takes away your suffering, your pains, and your diseases. He is the same yesterday, today, and forever.

> *God is not a man, that he should lie; neither the son of man, that he should repent: hath he said, and shall he not do it? or hath he spoken, and shall he not make it good?*
>
> — Numbers 23:19

God can do what He says He can do, and that is what faith is. Faith is very simple. Faith is believing that God can do what He says He can do. Many people struggle with faith, and they believe that they can never have faith. I ask them a very simple question, "Do you believe God can do what He says He can do?" I ask you the same question. The answer is what faith is. If you believe it, then that is what faith is. God can raise the dead, and God can heal.

The Healing God

Every redemptive name of God was given to Him by men who encountered Him. When Moses encountered God, he called Him "Jehovah Nissi." When Gideon encountered God, he called Him "Jehovah Shalom, the God of my peace." When Abraham encountered God, He called Him "Jehovah Jireh, the God my provider." But God called Himself a healer by His own will by giving Himself the name "Jehovah Rapha, God the healer." "I am the Lord that healeth thee." You do not agonize or beg God for healing. Healing is who He is.

I remember T.L. Osborn told a story. He said the first time he started to hear about healing, to read and study about it, he was going to have his first healing service. So, he announced on the radio and everywhere for people to bring the sick. People were going to come, and the reality of what he had done hit him, and he became afraid. He decided he was going to go on a fast for 10 days.

He told his wife, "I am going to go into that room for 10 days. Don't let me out. I am going to pray and ask God to heal." He locked himself in, and when he was there, he prayed, "God, when the sick come and I lay my hands on the sick, please heal them." He said he was begging from the first day. He kept begging and begging on the second day. On the third day, as he continued begging, suddenly, he said he heard the voice of God echo back from heaven to him saying, "For me?" the Lord said to him, "T.L., are you trying to convince me to heal the sick? Before you were ever interested in healing, I was interested. Before you ever had a passion for healing, I did something about it. I sent My son 2,000 years ago. He died for them and was bruised for their sickness and diseases." He called Himself a healer of His own will. God was interested before you knew anything about healing.

Chapter Two

This Same Jesus!

Jesus Christ the same yesterday, and to day, and for ever.

— Hebrews 13:8

I am excited to write this chapter because this verse is my favorite scripture. I preach it everywhere I go. Most of the crusades I have conducted were called "The Same Jesus." This is because I believe that people today need to see Jesus the same way people in Bible days saw Him. What do I mean by this? The people in Bible days saw Jesus as the Healer. The woman with the issue of blood knew that if she could only touch the hem of His garment, she would be made whole. The centurion knew that if Jesus would only speak a word, his servant would be healed. Martha knew that if Jesus had been there, Lazarus would not have died. Jairus knew that if Jesus would only touch his daughter, she would live. That is how they saw Him in Bible days. Is He the same today?

Joseph Achanya

I am so glad that Jesus has not changed! This is the foundation for miracles. If we do not believe in miracles, then we do not believe in Hebrews 13:8. That is why I can confidently stand in an intellectual world with many "alternatives" to miracles and say that I believe in miracles. The miracles that we see everywhere we go are proof that He has not changed. I am a witness that He is alive today!

I was preaching at a healing meeting in Oklahoma when a young girl, about twelve years old, who was partially blind, interrupted the service. She began to scream, "Pray for me! I want to see!" I stopped preaching, walked to her, and laid my hands on her eyes. Then, I commanded, "Spirit of blindness, come out of her!" When I took my hands off her eyes, she began to scream, "I can see! I can see!" Her eyes were completely healed! Hallelujah! Jesus is unchanged today! Bible days are here again. Just as blind Bartimaeus interrupted Jesus' service and his eyes were opened! At another crusade in Obi, Nigeria, a woman brought her daughter to me for prayer. She said that a spirit came on her when she was just 2 months old and since then, she has been deaf and mute for 16 years, just like Mark 9:17.

> *One of the men in the crowd spoke up and said,*
> *"Teacher, I brought my son so you could heal him.*
> *He is possessed by an evil spirit that won't let him*
> *talk."*
>
> *— Mark 9:17 (NLT)*

People think that we don't need miracles today because the world is now advanced. But that's not true. There are still as many sick people today as there were in Bible days. People still suffer the same disease today as the people in Bible days.

But the good news is that we have power over the Devil today, just like Jesus did in Bible days!

> *When Jesus saw that the people came running together, he rebuked the foul spirit, saying unto him, Thou dumb and deaf spirit, I charge thee, come out of him, and enter no more into him. And the spirit cried, and rent him sore, and came out of him: and he was as one dead; insomuch that many said, He is dead.*
>
> — Mark 9:25-26

The same authority came on me while I was on the platform. I commanded the spirit of deafness to come out of the young girl, and she was healed! The people surrounding her ran up to the platform shouting, "She's talking! She's talking!" No theologian can convince me that Jesus has changed. My eyes have seen it, and I know it as a fact.

His Word Is the Same Today

Everything written in the Bible remains unchanged from when it was first written. If the sick were healed in Bible days when Jesus commanded it, then the sick can take Jesus at His word today and be healed. Jesus spoke, and the dead returned to life! With just one word of His command, the crippled walked! Demons left their victims just by a single order, and even the deaf heard His voice! Is He still the same today?

His Ministry Is the Same Today

> *This beginning of miracles did Jesus in Cana of Galilee,*

> *and manifested forth his glory; and his disciples believed on him.*
>
> — John 2:11

> *The Spirit of the Lord is upon me, because he hath anointed me to preach the gospel to the poor; he hath sent me to heal the brokenhearted, to preach deliverance to the captives, and recovering of sight to the blind, to set at liberty them that are bruised,*
>
> — Luke 4:18

These are scriptural records about the beginning of the anointed miracle ministry of Jesus. However, there is no single scriptural reference about the end of His miracle ministry. Nowhere does it say, "The days of miracles are over" or "Miracles ended with the last apostle." The same Jesus who walked the streets of Jerusalem is alive today! And He is doing the same things He did in Bible days! If we do not believe that, then we don't believe the Bible. He was a miracle worker then, and He is a miracle worker now!

His Mission Is the Same Today

> *How God anointed Jesus of Nazareth with the Holy Ghost and with power: who went about doing good, and healing all that were oppressed of the devil; for God was with him.*
>
> — Acts 10:38

Jesus is still going about doing good. His thoughts for you are still good. His will is still good. His mission to heal you from the oppression of the devil and His compassion for the sick is still the same. He loves you, and He wants to help you.

His Power Is the Same Today

And he said, The things which are impossible with men are possible with God.

— Luke 18:27

Jesus has not lost His power as many have imagined. Many say, "I wished we lived in Bible days." But this is the hour for greater works! This is the hour of the resurrected Christ! Nothing is impossible with God! After a miracle service we had in Texas, a lady tearfully said, "It was as if we were in Bible days, and Jesus was walking in our midst." She said this because of the miracle she had just witnessed. His power is unchanged today.

A blind man will have no interest in the story of blind Bartimaeus if Jesus cannot open blind eyes today. Jesus Christ of Nazareth has become Jesus Christ of your city, your home, and your life today! That's good news if you need a miracle. What will happen to your disease in the presence of Jesus Christ? It will die, and you will be free!

Chapter Three

The Origin of Sickness and Disease

From the Beginning, It Was Not So

If you want to know God's original plan, go back to the very beginning. In Eden, we see God's intention for you. God had an idea to make man whole without sickness or disease. Man's eyes were made to see. His legs were made to walk, and his ears were made to hear.

> *And the Lord God formed man of the dust of the ground, and breathed into his nostrils the breath of life; and man became a living soul.*
>
> — Genesis 2:7

"The breath of life," not the breath of death! God did not breathe cancer into you; cancer takes life away from you. That's not from the breath of life. Your body was not made as a temple of disease; your body was made as a temple of the Holy Ghost! Whatever takes life away from you is not God's plan.

> *And God saw every thing that he had made, and,*
> *behold, it was very good. And the evening and the*
> *morning were the sixth day.*
>
> — Genesis 1:31

Everything God makes is good. If it comes from God, you know that it's good. Then you must ask yourself this question, is cancer good? Is diabetes good? Is kidney failure good? Is heart disease good? No! None of these are from God. They are intruders. They have no right to be in your body. Resist it! If I sound angry while I am preaching, it is because I know that sickness is not right. God wants them to be whole, just like He made them.

That Old Serpent

> *And the great dragon was cast out, that old serpent,*
> *called the Devil, and Satan, which deceiveth the*
> *whole world: he was cast out into the earth, and*
> *his angels were cast out with him.*
>
> — Revelation 12:9

So the question we have to answer is, "If it was not so from the beginning, what happened?" Why sicknesses? Why diseases? Why death? Where did it come from? It's from that old serpent called the Devil. Eden was perfect until Satan found his way there. The Bible calls him a deceiver. He succeeded in deceiving Eve into disobeying God. He said to her, "Go ahead and disobey God. It won't hurt you." That's the same way he is deceiving the whole world today. His tricks have not changed. He is still saying the same thing,

"Go ahead and sin, it won't hurt you." But sin brings death. Adam and Eve activated the law of sin and death when they disobeyed God.

> *For the wages of sin is death; but the gift of God is eternal life through Jesus Christ our Lord.*
>
> *— Romans 6:23*

Suddenly everything began to die. Now, the body will start to grow weak, the eyes grow dim, hearing fades, and the heart stops functioning. The Devil is the origin of all sickness and all disease.

War in Heaven

> *And there was war in heaven: Michael and his angels fought against the dragon; and the dragon fought and his angels, And prevailed not; neither was their place found any more in heaven. And the great dragon was cast out, that old serpent, called the Devil, and Satan, which deceiveth the whole world: he was cast out into the earth, and his angels were cast out with him. And I heard a loud voice saying in heaven, Now is come salvation, and strength, and the kingdom of our God, and the power of his Christ: for the accuser of our brethren is cast down, which accused them before our God day and night. And they overcame him by the blood of the Lamb, and by the word of their testimony; and they loved not their lives unto the death. Therefore rejoice, ye heavens, and ye that dwell in them. Woe to the inhabiters of the earth and of the*

> *sea! for the devil is come down unto you, having great wrath, because he knoweth that he hath but a short time.*
>
> — Revelation 12:7-12

Can you imagine a war in heaven? Wherever the Devil is, there's chaos. Eden was perfect until he came, and heaven was perfect once he was kicked out. He is the thief Jesus talks about in John 10:10 who comes to steal, kill, and destroy. When the Devil was cast out of heaven, the Bible says that heaven rejoiced. But there was a warning to those on the earth because he came down in great anger. I hear people say all the time, "If God is good, then why is there so much evil on the earth?" We find the answer in that scripture. It is not just God and man in the equation. There is an adversary named the Devil.

Spirit of Infirmity

> *How God anointed Jesus of Nazareth with the Holy Ghost and with power: who went about doing good, and healing all that were oppressed of the devil; for God was with him.*
>
> — Acts 10:38

God doesn't use sickness to teach you a lesson. It is an oppression from the Devil. That's why when you hear us pray for the sick, we rebuke Satan. For almost every sick person Jesus healed, He first rebuked the spirit behind it. Jesus said, "Thou deaf and dumb spirit..." (Mark 9:25). I want to give

Signs and Wonders Follow You

you another example from the Bible. Let's look at Luke 13:10-13.

> *And he was teaching in one of the synagogues on the sabbath. And, behold, there was a woman which had a spirit of infirmity eighteen years, and was bowed together, and could in no wise lift up herself. And when Jesus saw her, he called her to him, and said unto her, Woman, thou art loosed from thine infirmity. And he laid his hands on her: and immediately she was made straight, and glorified God.*
>
> — Luke 13:10-13

For 18 years, she was bent over. I am sure that in 18 years, she went to many physicians just like the woman with the issue of blood. The doctors may have diagnosed her condition as arthritis. That is what they could see, but the real origin was the spirit of infirmity. You may have a diagnosis from a doctor. I have a diagnosis from the Bible. The origin of sickness is the Devil!

The moment the spirit was cast out of her, she was healed! There lies the answer. When the Devil was cast down from heaven, joy was restored in heaven. So also, when the spirit of infirmity departs from you, your health will be restored to you. When Jesus was questioned about the woman's healing, He replied, "And ought not this woman, being a daughter of Abraham, whom Satan hath bound, lo, these eighteen years, be loosed from this bond on the sabbath day?" (Luke 13:16). Satan, that old serpent. It was his doing that held her bound for 18 years. But who the Son sets free, is free indeed!

Joseph Achanya

But Job?

How about Job? Was his sickness from God? I say let the theologians keep quiet and let the Bible answer.

> *So went Satan forth from the presence of the Lord, and smote Job with sore boils from the sole of his foot unto his crown.*
>
> — Job 2:7

It was him again, that old serpent! He smote Job. The Devil can no more hide, we found him. Wherever we find sickness and disease, we find him behind the scenes. One of the Devil's strategies is to smite people with sickness and convince them that it came from God. There are people all over the world angry at God, like Job's wife, because God was misinterpreted. God wants you well, it's the Devil that wants you sick. God wants you to live, it's the Devil that wants you to die. God wants you to prosper, it's the Devil that wants you to suffer.

> *After the Lord had finished speaking to Job, he said to Eliphaz the Temanite: "I am angry with you and your two friends, for you have not spoken accurately about me, as my servant Job has."*
>
> — Job 42:7 (NLT)

You do not speak accurately of God when you say that God put sickness on you to teach you a lesson. Satan smote Job, and God healed him.

> *When Job prayed for his friends, the Lord restored his*

fortunes. In fact, the Lord gave him twice as much as before!

— Job 42:10 (NLT)

The Devil was the adversary, God IS the Healer! Resist the Devil right now. Say, "Satan! You have no rights in my body! You are no longer my master. Loosen me NOW in Jesus' Name!"

Chapter Four

Creative Miracles

The subject of miracles is crucial. If I were to put out a prayer request today asking who would like me to pray for them and what they would want me to pray about, you would find that about 50 percent or more would request prayer for healing. They would seek healing in their bodies, minds, and other aspects.

Many people are sick, dying, oppressed, and possess the spirit of infirmity. This is an important topic to address.

When we talk about healing, we find that many people actually believe in it. Whether it's headaches, back pain, leg pain, or a wound, we believe God can heal all of these. However, when we encounter more severe conditions like a broken bone, a missing body part, or a completely non-functional organ, we start to question, "Can God do anything about it?" This includes illnesses considered incurable by doctors. I have seen a child born without eyeballs, another without eardrums, and another with a single testicle. Despite this, many still wonder, "Can God do anything about this?"

We believe God can perform other miracles, but when we encounter creative miracles, we begin to doubt God's ability to address sickness. Let me say this now: God is indifferent to whether it is leg pain or a missing leg. To God, it is all the same; it only requires His creative power. God is unconcerned whether it is a liver problem or a missing liver. He is indifferent. He is unconcerned if it is a cataract in the eye or no eyeballs at all. He is indifferent because, with God, all things are possible (Matthew 19:26). God does not sit in heaven and say a condition is too much for Him to handle. He doesn't care if it is paralysis or a completely missing body part. When it comes to the subject of creative miracles, I would like to start from where the Bible first began—with God's creative power.

> *In the beginning God created the heavens and the earth.*
>
> — Genesis 1:1 (NLT)

It is as simple as it is written: God made the heavens and the earth. If you ever doubt God's power to perform creative miracles, go to Genesis 1:1. Have you seen the wonders of the earth? Science talks about the Seven Wonders of the World, such as the Great Pyramid of Giza and the Hanging Gardens of Babylon. It blows your mind away. The Bible says that in the beginning, God made that. God created the heavens and the earth.

I must establish here that science doesn't create. This is where people make a mistake. Science doesn't create; it only discovers. It is all about discovery. Science looks at what God made and fashions a discovery. For example, think about the airplane. Science didn't create the law of gravity that makes the plane fly. Science didn't create the law of thrust and the four laws that govern flight. It only discovered the laws and, with their discovery, made an invention. Science doesn't create; it only discovers. Only God creates.

Every invention is governed by different laws, including light. Every scientific invention is governed by laws created by God. This is where God's creative power can be recognized. In the beginning, God created the heavens and the earth.

> *God created everything through Him, and nothing was created except through Him.*
>
> — John 1:3 (NLT)

One day, I was praying, and God echoed this scripture back to me. He said, "If you ever forget anything about Me, don't ever forget that by Me was all things made, and without Me was nothing made that was made." All things were made by God.

When we start to get into the details of creative miracles, think of the man called Moses. God spoke to Moses in Exodus chapter 4, telling him He was going to use him to deliver the Israelites. In verse 10 (NLT), Moses replied,

> *O Lord, I'm not very good with words. I never have been, and I'm not now, even though You have spoken to me. I get tongue-tied, and my words get tangled.*

Moses was telling God that he was born with the infirmity of stuttering and would never be able to speak. Let's look at verse 11 (NLT), which is one of the greatest revelations of miracles that I know. This is a scripture never to forget. The Word says,

> *Then the LORD asked Moses, Who makes a person's mouth? Who decides whether people speak or do not speak, hear or do not hear, see or do not see? Is it not I, the LORD?*

This verse covers three kinds of infirmity: dumbness, deafness, and blindness. God asked, "Who makes a person's mouth? Who decides whether a person speaks or does not speak? Who decides whether a person hears or does not hear? And who decides whether a person sees or does not see? Is it not I, the LORD?" God is speaking of His creative power.

God told Moses that He alone decides if the mouth can speak. God made the legs. He could decide if the legs could work or not. God made the head, fingers, lungs, liver, womb, intestine, spinal cord, neck, and veins. We could go on and on. Whatever body part you can remember, God made them all, and He says, "I decide!" God is preaching His message by Himself. I am not speaking for God; He is saying it Himself. So, when I am faced with someone who has a missing body part, I am certain God can heal them. If you are reading this book right now and you have a missing body part, and you ask, "Can God heal me?" God is answering you and He is saying, "Who made that body part? Who made it?" He says, "I decide."

God speaks of His creative power Himself. This is why in Matthew 15:30, the Word says,

> *And great multitudes came unto him, having with them those that were lame, blind, dumb, maimed, and many others, and cast them down at Jesus' feet; and he healed them.*

Signs and Wonders Follow You

I am shocked that many translations took the word "maimed" out of this verse. Are they doubting God's power? To be maimed means to have a body part damaged. So, the Bible verse says they brought to Jesus those who were maimed, that is, those whose body parts had been permanently damaged. Their eyes, legs, and back were permanently removed. What did the Bible say next? It says Jesus healed them all! God doesn't care about infirmity. What we have can heal anybody of anything. The dumb, blind, lame, and the maimed are all in the same category, and Jesus healed them all. Jesus performed a creative miracle. He even grew out legs.

Think of the Roman soldier's ear. When Jesus was to be arrested, Peter took out a sword and cut off the ear of one of the Roman soldiers. What did Jesus do? He picked up the ear from the floor and put it back on the soldier, and it was sealed (Luke 22:50-51). That was a creative miracle. This was what God said to Moses, "Who made the ear?"

Let me ask you this question: if I were to give an altar call right now and five people stepped forward to answer it, and one had told a lie, another had committed adultery, another was a child trafficker, one was a drunkard, and the last was an armed robber, would you consider these to be different categories of sin based on their degree of severity? You might ask, "Does sin have degrees?" Jesus said that Pilate committed a greater sin (John 19:11), which suggests the existence of different degrees of sin. If all five of these people answer the altar call and believe in their hearts that the blood of Jesus cleanses them from their sins, and I say the prayer of salvation with them, they would all believe that they are saved, cleansed, and forgiven by God. Everyone believes this, no matter the denomination. Everyone believes that no matter the sin committed, when you come to the altar, God can forgive you. However, when the topic shifts to miracles, and I call for a healing line with people presenting different categories of sicknesses and diseases, doubt suddenly arises regarding which of these God will heal and which He will not. We begin to question which infirmities God will heal instantly and which ones will take more time.

The question then becomes, why don't we do that with sin? Why do we do that with sickness? With God, all things are possible! (Matthew 19:26). God doesn't care if it is just pain in the back or no spinal cord at all. He doesn't care. With God, all things are possible!

I enjoy applying the same principles Baptists use to discuss salvation to the topic of miracles. Just as Baptists believe in the possibility of salvation for all, I believe that with God, all things are possible, regardless of the severity of the sickness or disease.

In Jeremiah 18:1-6 (NLT), the scripture says, "The LORD gave another message to Jeremiah. He said, 'Go down to the potter's shop, and I will speak to you there.' So I did as He told me and found the potter working at his wheel. But the jar he was making did not turn out as he had hoped, so he crushed it into a lump of clay again and started over. Then the LORD gave me this message: 'O Israel, can I not do to you as this potter has done to his clay? As the clay is in the potter's hand, so are you in my hand.'"

This is a fundamental discovery. What was man created from? In the first chapter of Genesis, it is stated that man was formed from the dust (clay). This is a revelation about God and man, and God is saying, "Look! As clay is in the hand of the potter, so are you in my hand." If anything goes wrong in your body, He is saying He can remold a new one for you. New eardrums, new lenses in the eyes for you to see clearly again, or completely new red blood cells. We have seen SS turn to AA in our crusades. God can put new blood cells in anybody. This is why I am not afraid to pray for anybody. You could bring me someone who is completely divided into two, and I am still going to pray. I believe with God all things are possible.

One time, Archbishop Benson Idahosa was preaching in his church, The Miracle Cathedral, when a child fell from the top of the building and hit the ground, splitting their head in front of everyone. He kept preaching as though he didn't see it, and the whole crowd was going wild because of the incident. The Archbishop walked to the child, put his two hands on their head, prayed, and instantly, the wound closed up in front of everyone, and he continued preaching. If you don't believe that, then you don't believe the Bible, because Jesus took the Roman soldier's ear from the ground, put it back, and it was healed. This is the Bible. Creative miracles can happen.

God said, "Can I not do this with you? Can I not mold you again? Can I not mold new body parts?" God can create everything new. There is hope for amputees. God can create new legs and new arms. It happened with Paul, Peter, and in the Bible days, and it can still happen today. This is why I believe that with God, all things are possible. Praise the Lord!

If you come to me about prayer, it doesn't matter what you say, I am going to pray. There is hope for amputees, and I have prayed for amputees before. There is a viral video where they were mocking a preacher who was going to pray for someone who was lame and his legs were covered. The preacher took off the blanket and saw that the guy had no legs at all, and everybody around made fun and laughed. It wasn't funny to me. With God, all things are possible. I say,

Joseph Achanya

"With God, all things are possible!" Everybody laughed at this preacher. Were they trying to say that with God, not all things are possible? Just because the man doesn't have legs, God can't do anything? I say again, with much emphasis, with God, all things are possible!

Chapter Five

You Can Be Sure

In this chapter, I want to share a truth that I know gives me faith in the subject of healing. The Bible says, *"You will know the truth, and the truth will set you free"* (John 8:32 NLT). There is a truth that I know about the subject of healing that gives me faith. This truth inspires and stirs my faith when I stand in front of a sick person.

> *Surely he hath borne our griefs, and carried our sorrows: yet we did esteem him stricken, smitten of God, and afflicted. But he was wounded for our transgressions, he was bruised for our iniquities: the chastisement of our peace was upon him; and with his stripes we are healed.*
>
> — Isaiah 53:4-5

It began by saying "surely." Do you know what that word means? It means that you can be sure about it. It's a fact. It's the same way Jesus starts His parables with "verily, verily" when speaking to His disciples. The word "verily" also means "surely." This means that it is a fact, and it is the same with Isaiah 53:4-5.

So many people are not sure about the year they were born. If you were born in Africa before the 60s, there was no calendar, and some people do not know when they were born. Their parents told them they were born when a certain president died or in the year of a specific event. This pattern also happened in Bible days. The Bible says, "In the year that King Uzziah died, Isaiah saw..." (Isaiah 6:1). This is how the calendar was. The death of a prominent person was used, and that was how people knew their age back then. But that is not a fact. They were not sure about that. There are so many things people are not sure about. However, by using the word "surely," Isaiah said in Isaiah 53:4-5, "Concerning what I am about to tell you, you can be sure about it. It is a fact."

Now, what is he talking about? I will give you four facts from what Isaiah talked about. This is the first fact: "He Himself" "Surely he hath borne..." You can be sure it wasn't a prophet, Moses, Elijah, Deborah, or any of the judges of the Old Testament. You can be sure that it was Jesus Himself who took our pains. When God saw the children of Israel in bondage, He wanted to deliver them, and He sent Moses. Throughout the Old Testament, we saw that the children of Israel went back into bondage, and God sent a judge. There were several judges like Deborah and Samson. But Isaiah started by prophesying that the word he was talking about wasn't done by Elijah or any of the prophets. You can be sure it was Jesus Christ of Nazareth Himself who took our pain. When God wanted to deliver the entire human race, He came down Himself. A translation says, "He Himself took our pains." You can be sure about that. It's a fact. If you read Revelation 1:18, Jesus Christ introduced Himself as "He that was dead and now I am alive." He introduced Himself as the person whom Isaiah prophesied about, saying, "I am He." If you want to know if Jesus was indeed the one Isaiah was talking about, read Matthew 8:16-17. When Jesus began to perform miracles, Matthew said all the miracles He did were to fulfill what the prophet Isaiah talked about, that He Himself took our infirmities. So, you can be sure that it was Jesus Christ of Nazareth who took our pains.

The second thing you can be sure of is the fact that it was your pain that He took. "Surely he hath borne our griefs, and carried our sorrows..." The word "our" includes you. Psalm 103:1-3 says: "Bless the LORD, O my soul: and all that is within me, bless his holy name. Bless the LORD, O my soul, and forget not all his benefits: Who forgiveth all thine iniquities; who healeth all thy diseases." When he said "our," does that include you? Yes, it does! You can be sure about that. You can be specific and mention whatever disease, pain, or iniquity He took. It was your cancer, diabetes, eye problem, cataract, leg pain, glaucoma, paralysis, or stroke that He took. You can be sure that "our" includes you. Jesus did not die for the multitude; He died for individuals. He had every single person in mind when He died, and that includes you.

The third thing you can be sure about is that your pains and sufferings are gone. "Surely he hath borne our griefs, and carried our sorrows..." If Jesus took your pain and suffering, where does that leave you? It leaves you without any pain. You can be sure about that. This is what redemption is about. What is redemption? Redemption is whatever Jesus did on the cross that I do not have to do anymore. Whatever He suffered with on the cross, you don't have to deal with anymore. The price that was paid on the cross was vicarious. In the next chapter, I will talk more about redemption in its fullness. You can be sure that your pain, suffering, transgressions, iniquities, and wounds are all gone. It's all gone, and it leaves you without any pain, diseases, and suffering. Why do you have to suffer anymore if Jesus suffered for you? Why do you have to live in pain anymore if Jesus took your pains? You can be sure that the cross was a painkiller. He took it. This is a fact.

The fourth fact you can be sure about is that you are healed. "...and with his stripes we are healed." You may say to yourself, "But I do not feel healed." The first verse of Isaiah 53 begins by saying, "Who hath believed our report?" The same way your doctor came to you and pronounced that you had cancer, or three months to live, or you had leukemia, the same way the doctor came with his pronouncement is the same way Isaiah came with his. He is saying that if you believe this report, you can be sure that you are healed! It is a report from the Lord. So, what are you waiting for? How can the devil keep you sick if Jesus says you are healed? Remember, God's Word is a statement of fact. When God speaks, it is a fact. You are who God says you are. If God says you are healed, why do you say you are not healed? If God says your pain is gone, why do you still have it? God's Word is a statement of fact. You can help yourself right now and get up and walk. Break loose from your captors today. You are healed!

God's Word is the fact. You can only remain afflicted if you believe the devil more than you believe God. But if you believe that divine healing is greater than devils and diseases, they will all disappear. The Bible says that God watches over His words to perform it (Jeremiah 1:12). God is watching over His word to perform it for anyone who can say, "I believe." If you can believe this fact, you can be sure to receive your healing.

It is because of these facts that I know there are certain results I expect when I pray for the sick. The Bible says you shall lay your hands on the sick, and the sick shall recover (Mark 16:18). That is a fact. They can recover because you can be sure that He has carried their sickness away. I can be sure about that, and this is why wherever I go, I expect that the sick shall be healed. This is why I expect that whosoever shall call upon the name of the Lord shall be saved (Romans 10:13). It is why I expect that whosoever believes in Him shall not perish but have everlasting life (John 3:16). These are all facts. He that believes in Him shall be saved, shall have life, shall recover, and shall not die. Why? Because I can be sure that He Himself took our (which includes you) infirmities, and with His stripes, you are healed.

Chapter Six

The Realities Of Redemption

*Christ hath redeemed us from the curse of the law,
being made a curse for us.*

— Galatians 3:13

This opening scripture is essential. "Us" here means you and me. If this is true, then it means we are redeemed. Note that it is not "I am going to be redeemed," or "Christ is planning to redeem me," or "My redemption is coming," but "Christ hath redeemed us." Redemption is a fact.

What does it mean to be redeemed? It means "to buy back what is lost or stolen." Christ has bought you back. It means "to be ransomed by paying a debt." It means to be set free from captivity and to be loosed from bondage.

Take a moment and imagine losing your pet, and someone finds it and takes it to the animal shelter. Later, you find out where it is. You go there, but you cannot have it for free; you have to pay to redeem it. You paid to redeem your lost property. So when you say you have been redeemed, that is your story. If you are a prisoner of sickness, afflictions, bondage, or anything contrary to God's will, the Bible says that Christ has redeemed you.

Understand that God believes in, dreams about, and plans for your freedom. We see this in Exodus 3:6-7 (NLT), where He says, "I am the God of your father—the God of Abraham, the God of Isaac, and the God of Jacob." When Moses heard this, he covered his face because he was afraid to look at God. Then the Lord told him, "I have certainly seen the oppression of my people in Egypt."

God has seen your needs, problems, bondage, and captivity, and He says, "I believe in freedom. I do not want you to be bound and in chains. I have come down to deliver you." It was God who made the birds to fly freely and the fish to swim freely. He believes in freedom, and He made man to be free as well. He made man to live without limitations, reaching as high as he wants to reach.

This is why we have fundamental human rights, such as freedom of speech. These are freedoms that God wants us to enjoy. God believes in freedom, not bondage, chains, or addictions. He made you free, just like the birds of the air. The idea of freedom concerns God because many of His people have been sold as slaves to all kinds of influences. They have been bound by medication, masturbation, pornography, the spirit of lust, and many other influences. If you hear what people struggle with in secret, you will be amazed. It is as though the devil puts them on an auction and they have been sold to captivity. Different spirits have bid and bought them, but God says that is not His dream for them.

Imagine a man who has a market and sees that he does not have enough people visiting his market. He decides to buy an eagle and put it in front of his store, which becomes a center of attraction. When people come to see the eagle, they hang around and get something from his store. People see the eagle by the store, come inside, buy items, and leave. This continues for many years. Then one day, someone walks into the store and sees the eagle in the cage. This person, a lover of nature, knows that an eagle being in a cage is not right. It is supposed to be a free bird meant to fly as high as it can go. He walks to the owner of the store and makes his intentions known about buying the eagle. The owner of the store doesn't want to sell the eagle, so he thinks to himself, "I will mention a very high and ridiculous price so this man can leave." He tells the man the price, and you know what the man responds? He says, "I will buy it. I will sell everything that I have. I will empty my savings account and buy this eagle." He eventually buys the eagle, and everyone wonders what he will do with the eagle. In front of them, he opens the eagle's cage, brings it out, and lets it fly freely. One of the onlookers asks him, "Why did you let it go? You bought it for a high price." The man responds, "An eagle shouldn't be caged; it should be left to fly high to the mountains."

This is what God did for you. He said to Himself, "You shouldn't be bound in chains and in captivity." He sold all that He had. He gave His very best to redeem you from your infirmities and captivity. He came down to the slave market and auction party for you, and He said, "No more. I will buy you back. You were mine from the beginning. I made you to be free." God believes in redemption.

Jesus came preaching freedom.

> *The Spirit of the Lord is on me because He has anointed me to proclaim good news to the poor. He has sent me to proclaim freedom for the prisoners and*

> *recovery of sight for the blind, to set the oppressed free.*
>
> — Luke 4:18 (NIV)

This was the first message Jesus ever preached. He preached the gospel of freedom. "You ought not to be bound," He said. If you are oppressed by any sickness, addiction, and are a prisoner of the devil, I am glad to announce to you that you are already free. Jesus said you do not have to be in bondage anymore. Freedom was His message, not bondage. Freedom is the message of the Kingdom. This is what the gospel is. The gospel is the announcement of God's redemptive blessings, and the first redemptive blessing is freedom. One time, Jesus saw a donkey tied and said, "Loose it and let it go." Another time, He saw Lazarus tied and bound, and He said to them, "Loose him and let him go." This is His message: "Loose him! Loose her!"

I believe in doctors, but the Bible said, "There is a more excellent way" (1 Corinthians 12:31). This was what Jesus came to announce. It was God's message to Pharaoh: "Let My people go! You have bound them too long. They have been oppressed too long. Loose them and let My people go!" (Exodus 5:1). That has been God's message from the beginning, and it is still Jesus' message today—freedom for all.

> *He saw a woman who had been crippled by an evil spirit. She had been bent double for eighteen years and was unable to stand up straight. When Jesus saw her, he called her over and said, 'Dear woman, you are healed of your sickness!' Then he touched her, and instantly she could stand straight.*
>
> — Luke 13:11-13 (NLT)

Signs and Wonders Follow You

If sickness and disease are the same today as they were in Bible days, then Jesus is the same today as He was in Bible days. If the same spirit that bound people in Bible days is still present on earth binding people, then why should Jesus change? Why do people say Jesus is no longer at work today when these spirits, contrary to redemption, are at work?

Spirits don't change their agenda; it is always the same. It is oppression. The same spirit was against Elijah. Jezebel prophesied that she would cut off the head of Elijah and put it on a platter. Jezebel was the wife of King Ahab, and Elijah was God's prophet. She died without fulfilling her agenda. Many years later, there was another prophet named John the Baptist, and the Bible recorded that John came in the spirit and likeness of Elijah (Luke 1:17). My question then is: how did John the Baptist die? His head was cut off and put on a platter. Who ordered the execution of John the Baptist? It was the wife of the king. It was an agenda in the spirit that never died out; the spirits are all the same. If the spirits don't change, why should Jesus change? Why should healing not be for today if people are still sick today? Has God lost His compassion? Does God care more for people in Bible days than for people today?

> *Through Christ Jesus, God has blessed the Gentiles with the same blessing he promised to Abraham, so that we who are believers might receive the promised Holy Spirit through faith.*
>
> — Galatians 3:14 (NLT)

God said that He redeemed us so that we can be part of the blessing of Abraham. He also said that He doesn't care more for the Jews than He cares for the Gentiles and that He doesn't care for the people in the Bible days more than He cares for us today. Therefore, we are all redeemed.

> *On a Sabbath Jesus was teaching in one of the synagogues, and a woman was there who had been crippled by a spirit for eighteen years. She was bent over and could not straighten up at all. When Jesus saw her, he called her forward and said to her, 'Woman, you are set free from your infirmity.' Then he put his hands on her, and immediately she straightened up and praised God. Indignant because Jesus had healed on the Sabbath, the synagogue leader said to the people, 'There are six days for work. So come and be healed on those days, not on the Sabbath.' The Lord answered him, 'You hypocrites! Doesn't each of you on the Sabbath untie your ox or donkey from the stall and lead it out to give it water? Then should not this woman, a daughter of Abraham, whom Satan has kept bound for eighteen long years, be set free on the Sabbath day from what bound her?' When he said this, all his opponents were humiliated, but the people were delighted with all the wonderful things he was doing.*
>
> — Luke 13:10-17 (NIV)

I am sure if Jesus were here physically today, He would give the same response to people who say miracles are not for today. He would say that to people who say miracles passed away with the apostolic age. He is going to look at them and say, "You hypocrites! Don't you have pets? If you, being evil, know how to care for your pets, how much more your heav-

Signs and Wonders Follow You

enly Father?" Jesus called this woman a daughter of Abraham.

Remember Galatians 3:14, which says that the blessing of Abraham would come to the Gentiles through faith. This is the blessing of redemption.

When you say you are free, that is what the Bible affirms. It says you ought to be free. If you are deaf, you ought to hear. If you are blind, you ought to see. If you are paralyzed, you ought to walk. This is what Jesus came preaching. The redeemed are not supposed to be bound; the redeemed have been paid for. There is redeeming power in the name of Jesus to break every yoke. Embrace your freedom now.

"This dear woman, a daughter of Abraham, has been held in bondage by Satan for eighteen years. Isn't it right that she be released, even on the Sabbath?" (Luke 13:16 NLT). Jesus is saying here that if you are redeemed, then it is not right that you are still bound. Freedom is your blood-bought right. Break loose from your captors today. The prison door has been opened, and you can walk out today. Break loose from your bondage. The right to be released has been given to you.

The Holy Spirit is the Spirit of freedom.

> *Now the Lord is that Spirit: and where the Spirit of the Lord is, there is liberty.*
>
> — 2 Corinthians 3:17

God believes in freedom, Jesus announces freedom, and the Holy Spirit releases freedom. In Isaiah 10:27, the Bible says,

> *And it shall come to pass in that day, that his burden shall be taken away from off thy shoulder, and his*

> *yoke from off thy neck, and the yoke shall be*
> *destroyed because of the anointing.*

The anointing breaks every yoke. There is no sickness, disease, or oppression stronger than the anointing. The anointing breaks the yoke. The Holy Spirit is the Spirit of freedom, and where the Spirit of the Lord is, there is freedom.

In Acts 8, when Philip went to Samaria, under the anointing of the Holy Ghost, the Bible said unclean spirits and many demons cried and left their victims. Unclean spirits are still crying around the world and leaving their victims because of the anointing.

In Keffi, Nigeria, I held a crusade with about 5,000 people in attendance. At the crusade, I closed my eyes and prayed in tongues for fifteen minutes at the top of my voice in front of them all. When I opened my eyes, there were demons all over the front, screaming and crying. Demons and unclean spirits were crying out with a loud voice. The Holy Ghost is the Spirit of freedom.

Do you know what I tell people who don't believe in miracles today? I say to them, "While you are going around doing your podcasts and recording videos, I was going around the world proving that miracles are true." God believes in freedom. Jesus came announcing this freedom, and the Holy Spirit is the Spirit of freedom.

> *But ye shall receive power, after that the Holy Ghost is*
> *come upon you: and ye shall be witnesses unto me*
> *both in Jerusalem, and in all Judaea, and in*
> *Samaria, and unto the uttermost part of the earth.*
>
> — Acts 1:8

Every bondage is proof of the lack of power. You are bound when you do not want to be, say what you don't want to say, do what you don't want to do. Why? It is a lack of power. Where the Spirit of the Lord is, there is freedom.

You and I are ministers of freedom.

> *And he said unto them, Go ye into all the world, and preach the gospel to every creature.*
>
> — Mark 16:15

I am a minister of freedom, and this is what I go around the world doing. I set the captives free in that name that is above every other name. Another meaning of redemption is to cash out a voucher. Redemption is about redeeming points, just as with a voucher. We are both ministers of freedom.

Chapter Seven

Act Accordingly

For as the body without the spirit is dead, so faith without works is dead also.

— James 2:26

What is James saying here? He is saying that when you take the spirit out of a body, it becomes a dead body and of no use; it cannot produce. The spirit is what makes the body function. In comparison, he said that if you take action out of faith, it is equivalent to a dead body. Faith without action is dead faith.

You know what that tells me? There is living faith and dead faith. Living faith is active faith. A living faith acts accordingly. That is what defines faith. Instead of simply saying that you believe, demonstrate your faith through your actions. The Bible teaches us that faith is not just a matter of belief but also of action. In the Gospels, we see that Jesus often recognized and commended the faith of those who demonstrated it through their actions, as evidenced by the passage

"When Jesus saw their faith..." (Mark 2:5). When the four friends tore down the roof, the Bible mentions that Jesus saw their faith. This indicates that faith can be observed in action. The only faith that God honors is active faith.

Jesus asked, "How shall I liken this generation?" He continued, saying, "I piped to you, and you did not dance. I mourned, and you did not lament" (Matthew 11:17). This signifies that while He extends His hands, we fail to respond. When you come to the realization that the gospel is true, that Isaiah 53 holds truth in that He bore our infirmities, you then must demonstrate your belief through action.

If you say you are healed, then act like you are healed. If you say you believe the message, then respond. God is a faith God. The Bible says it is impossible to please God without faith. It does not say that you may please God or that there are other ways to please Him. It clearly states that without faith, it is impossible to please God. It is absolutely impossible to make God happy without faith.

The good news must first be announced, and the announcement of the good news must be embraced and acted upon. Action is what produces the miracle. If you read Acts 3, Peter and John went to the temple and stopped by the Beautiful Gate.

> *Now Peter and John went up together into the temple at the hour of prayer, being the ninth hour. And a certain man lame from his mother's womb was carried, whom they laid daily at the gate of the temple which is called Beautiful, to ask alms of them that entered into the temple; Who seeing Peter and John about to go into the temple asked an alms. And Peter, fastening his eyes upon him with*

Signs and Wonders Follow You

> *John, said, Look on us. And he gave heed unto them, expecting to receive something of them. Then Peter said, Silver and gold have I none; but such as I have give I thee: In the name of Jesus Christ of Nazareth rise up and walk. And he took him by the right hand, and lifted him up: and immediately his feet and ankle bones received strength. And he leaping up stood, and walked, and entered with them into the temple, walking, and leaping, and praising God.*

— Acts 3:1-8

Peter and John met this man who was lame from birth, and they said to him, "What we have is the Name of Jesus. In the Name of Jesus, we command you to get up and walk." Do you know what he was saying? He was saying, "In the name of Jesus, do what you couldn't do before I prayed. Get up and walk. You can't walk now, but you can walk after I pray." The man didn't respond. He kept staring at them, expecting a monetary gift. In verse 7, Peter took the man by his right hand and helped him up. Peter was simply saying, "Respond to my prayer! Put an action to your faith." They helped him up, and instantly, he was healed. Action makes faith work. Action proves that you believe it.

There are two aspects to Christianity: what you believe and what you do about what you believe. Many people stop at what they believe. However, what do you do about what you believe? Otherwise, Christianity and the Bible would remain stories and theories. It doesn't end there. What do you believe? I believe Isaiah 53:5,

> *But he was wounded for our transgressions, he was*

> *bruised for our iniquities: the chastisement of our peace was upon him; and with his stripes we are healed.*

That is what I believe, but what do I do with what I have believed? By His stripes, I am healed. If I am healed, then I must act like I am healed.

This is why when you read the book of Mark and see Jesus praying, He never said a prayer. When He met a blind person, He was only instructing him to do what they could not do before He encountered them.

> *Some men came, bringing to him a paralyzed man, carried by four of them. Since they could not get him to Jesus because of the crowd, they made an opening in the roof above Jesus by digging through it and then lowered the mat the man was lying on. When Jesus saw their faith, he said to the paralyzed man, 'Son, your sins are forgiven.' Now some teachers of the law were sitting there, thinking to themselves, Why does this fellow talk like that? He's blaspheming! Who can forgive sins but God alone?' Immediately Jesus knew in his spirit that this was what they were thinking in their hearts, and he said to them, Why are you thinking these things? Which is easier: to say to this paralyzed man, "Your sins are forgiven," or to say, "Get up, take your mat and walk"? But I want you to know that the Son of Man has authority on earth to forgive sins.' So he said to the man, 'I tell you, get up, take your mat and go home.'*
>
> — Mark 2:3-11 (NIV)

Jesus instructed the man to do what he could not do before. The man then took his bed and walked out, astonishing everyone. Consider what might have occurred if, following Jesus' command, the man had said, "Jesus, can't you see I am paralyzed?" However, he did not ask that. Instead, he rose, picked up his bed, and went home healed. You too can experience healing by taking action! The man demonstrated faith through action.

> *And he entered again into the synagogue; and there was a man there which had a withered hand. And they watched him, whether he would heal him on the Sabbath day; that they might accuse him. And he saith unto the man which had the withered hand, Stand forth. And he saith unto them, Is it lawful to do good on the Sabbath days, or to do evil? to save life, or to kill? But they held their peace. And when he had looked round about on them with anger, being grieved for the hardness of their hearts, he saith unto the man, Stretch forth thine hand. And he stretched it out: and his hand was restored whole as the other. And the Pharisees went forth, and straightway took counsel with the Herodians against him, how they might destroy him.*
>
> — Mark 3:1-6

The man stretched out his hand, and he was healed. Action is what makes faith work.

Paul encountered the same kind of miracle as Peter did in Acts 3. He also experienced a similar miracle to that of Jesus. While preaching, Paul noticed a man who was paying attention and believed. Recognizing the man's faith, Paul encouraged him to put his faith into action, saying, "Don't stop there. Put your faith into action." This message is one that I share with people worldwide whenever I preach, emphasizing the importance of both believing and actively demonstrating one's faith.

> *And there sat a certain man at Lystra, impotent in his feet, being a cripple from his mother's womb, who never had walked: The same heard Paul speak: who steadfastly beholding him, and perceiving that he had faith to be healed, Said with a loud voice, Stand upright on thy feet. And he leaped and walked.*
>
> — Acts 14:8-10

Paul was a powerful preacher with the anointing, but the man could have gone home paralyzed. Why? Faith without action is dead. The man got up, and he put his faith into action. Only believe and put your faith into action.

I was preaching in Texas, and at the close of the service, I was going to pray for the sick. A lady came to the service five days before the event. She had broken five discs in her back and could not walk. She arrived with a walker and was unable to do anything. I instructed the people in the congregation to place their hands where they were hurting. After my prayer, if they believed that God had heard me, they should attempt to do what they could not do before we prayed. I encouraged them to put their faith into action. They followed my instructions, and I prayed for God to restore them. As soon as I finished praying, the lady picked up her walker, lifted it onto her head, and for the first time in five days, she could walk

Signs and Wonders Follow You

again. By putting her faith into action, she experienced healing. In the words of Jesus, "Woman, your faith has made you well."

God is watching over His word to see people who will act on it as proof that they believe, and He will confirm it.

I tell people that the recipe for a miracle is simple:

1. Preach because the good news must first be announced.
2. You believe because the good news must be accepted.
3. I will talk to God because we can always expect a miracle from Him.
4. When I pray, I ask them to put their faith into action if they believe God has heard me.
5. God confirms.

Chapter Eight

Church Of Healing

The church is a place of healing.

Is any sick among you? let him call for the elders of the church; and let them pray over him, anointing him with oil in the name of the Lord.

— James 5:14

This was James' recommendation. The early church was a place of healing, not just for speech, talk, counseling, or storytelling. If anyone is sick, let them come to the church. This is why we have healing services; it is the Bible's recommendation. The church is God's clinic, where He performs His surgeries. Angels are positioned in the church, moving about and healing all who are oppressed by the devil.

The church is not a mosque or the temple of Buddha; it is the temple of Jesus. There is power in the church and in the gathering of believers.

Joseph Achanya

Where two or three are gathered in my name, I am
   there among them

— Matthew 18:20 (NRSV)

When people come to the church sick, they leave well. They come blind, they leave seeing. They come broken, they leave whole. They come hurting, they leave healed. They come sad, they leave with joy. They come bound, they leave free. They come tied, they leave untied.

The church is a place of signs, wonders, casting out of devils, and healing the sick. This is the great commission. Before Jesus left, He gave a great commission. He said,

Preach the gospel, heal the sick, raise the dead, and
   cast out devils in my name.

— Mark 16:15-18

Then He said that we will lay hands in His name, and the sick will recover. This is what we should expect in the church. The laying on of hands is not something we made up; it is the great commission.

A man came to one of my services where I laid hands on him. He said to me afterward, "I do not understand your laying of hands on me, but whatever you did, it worked." He couldn't explain it. I said I couldn't explain it either; it is called virtue. When the woman with the issue of blood touched Jesus, virtue came from Him and healed her. That is what happens when we lay hands on the sick. Healing virtue flows. The Bible says that you shall receive power after the Holy Ghost comes upon you (Acts 1:8). The same word translated as power is also translated as virtue. It is the same word "virtue" used when the woman with the issue of blood was healed by touching Jesus. The word "virtue" is the same as "dunamis," which means power. So, when the Bible says, "You shall receive power," you can interpret it to mean, "You shall receive virtue." When we lay hands on the sick, there is something that flows from Jesus and the cross, and it makes you well.

A man was brought to one of our services with a kidney problem and a urinary catheter, which he had been using for one year and six months due to his illness. During this period, he couldn't urinate properly. When we prayed the healing prayer and took testimonies, I noticed the man, whom I had never met before, coming forward to testify. He shared that he had been unable to urinate properly for one year and six months, relying on the catheter. While I was praying, he tapped his wife to take him to the bathroom. There, for the first time in one year and six months, he was able to urinate on his own. This occurred while I was still praying. Indeed, there is healing in the church!

When was the last time you heard of the dead rising? Is that too big for the church? We have been commanded to heal the sick and to raise the dead. It is what we should do without fear.

Chapter Nine

According To My Gospel

In this chapter, I would like to bear witness to the miraculous power of God across the nations, which is why I call it "My Gospel." Matthew wrote his gospel, detailing what he saw and experienced while traveling with Jesus. Mark provided his perspective on what he witnessed and experienced. John also wrote a gospel account, as did Luke, and an account was written of the Acts of the Apostles. Here is my gospel.

This is not an attempt to create a new gospel message, as the gospel message is the same everywhere. Instead, it is an effort to document what I have witnessed around the world. I will write about my experiences with the miracle worker, Jesus Christ.

I write to you today to proclaim that Jesus Christ is alive, and He remains the same yesterday, today, and forever. He continues to do the same things He did in the Bible days before He ascended into heaven. Today, I bear witness to many of the testimonies that we saw as miracle missionaries traveling around the world, preaching the gospel, casting out devils, setting the captives free, laying hands on the sick, and expecting them to recover.

A few months ago, we traveled to Botswana to conduct a Great Awakening Crusade in the city of Francistown. It was a four-day mass gospel campaign where people of all faiths and religions gathered from all over the city to hear me preach about Jesus. I had the opportunity to deliver a powerful message titled "The Power of God unto Salvation."

After the message, I called for a healing line for those who were sick and needed prayer for their ailments. A lady came forward who had been using crutches for many years and was struggling to walk. When she approached me, I laid my hands on her and commanded her, in the name of Jesus Christ of Nazareth, to rise up and walk. She stood up and began to walk with ease and perfection. Initially, I thought she may have only had a little pain in her back and was using the crutches for convenience, but it was clear that she had been healed. I then spoke with the lady and asked her what had happened. She said that she had been known for using crutches for many years and had become ashamed of it. However, when I laid my hands on her and she was healed, it was a life-changing experience for her. The next day, she returned to the crusade and shared her testimony with the entire crowd. She told them how she had walked the entire mall without her crutches to show everyone that she was a witness to the miracles of Jesus.

A few weeks after we left Botswana, she wrote a powerful testimony to me on Facebook, which I will share here:

> "Here I am as a living testimony from Botswana. I was in pain for too long using crutches to walk, but today I am walking with my own legs! No more crutches! For

Signs and Wonders Follow You

those who don't believe, I'm here to witness the mercy of God. Miracles do exist! I thank you. I believe God through the prayer of the man of God, and God did it for me! Be blessed, Evangelist, and may God use you more so those who do not believe will see and start to believe."

– Sean Wilson, Francistown, Botswana

That is a witness of one of the miracles that we saw in Francistown, Botswana. A few weeks later, when we left Botswana, we went to West Virginia in the United States. Here, we had a healing service on a Wednesday night. A lady came to the healing service, having suffered from a terrible condition. She had been diagnosed with three incurable diseases. I never knew she was there, but I prayed a mass healing prayer for everyone who suffered from different sicknesses and infirmities, instructing everyone to lay their hands on where they suffered. I said the prayer, and afterward, many came to share their testimonies.

A few days later, I received a wonderful testimony from the lady:

"Wednesday night during services with Preacher Jay, I received a healing in my back that was just wonderful. Through my years of pregnancy, especially when I carried my twins to term, unbeknownst to me, the whole muscle that surrounded my abdomen and went around my back was tearing. With subsequent pregnancies, it tore more, and I didn't realize it was happening. About ten years ago, a specialist told me that I was torn on both sides and it was not repairable. I had a very large abdominal hernia because of that,

and my spine was moving. It was unstable, and there
was nothing they could do about it. I could literally
feel my spine moving when I walked, and I didn't
realize my gait was changing because my spine was
moving so much. I was unsteady on my feet and
swayed as I walked, which I saw in videos. Preacher
Jay just asked us to stand at our seats and place our
hands where we needed healing. He began to pray, and
so did I. I felt the muscles around my back begin to
tighten. I began to walk back and forth. I could physically feel my healing. Wednesday was a powerful
service. The Holy Spirit was in this place, and I know
the key to my healing was a fresh indwelling of the
Holy Spirit. It had been moving in me all week, and
it's amazing the power available to God's people when
you pray in the Spirit, not in your own power.
"So, I want to tell you today that I am a living,
breathing testimony that my God is a God of more. He
didn't simply reach down and heal my back; He didn't
leave the rest of me broken. My hair has shed for
years, but in the last few years, it has fallen out in
clumps. Since Wednesday, not one hair has fallen out,
and that's more than I asked for! Also, I had several
skin cancers removed in the last year. One sore spot
on my ear, diagnosed as chondrodermatitis nodularis
helicis, was not healing. It was chronic and sore
because I slept on that side. My daughter bought me a
pillow with a hole in it because I could not sleep. Last
night, I realized my ear did not hurt. This morning,
there's no scab, and that's more than I asked for! I
don't know what else God has healed, but I look
forward every day to finding out! He is a good God,
and what He has done for me, I need you to know He
will do for you too. I zoomed around my office, and

everyone was amazed. I didn't realize how badly I walked, but they certainly noticed. I walked with such a swaying motion that my necklace would swing back and forth. It was embarrassing, and now it no longer swings."

A few weeks later, we went to a different city in West Virginia for a week-long meeting. During this meeting, a lady came to the service who had been blind in her left eye for sixty-five years. She was born blind in that eye. Sometimes, the condition was so bad that her eye would roll, showing the back instead of the front.

On the fifth night of the meeting, we had a healing and anointing service. She told me she had been blind in her left eye for sixty-five years. She had attended every night of the meeting where I preached on redemption. She was shy and didn't want to be in the spotlight, but she decided to come up because she wanted to be healed. I laid my hands on her eye with anointing oil, prayed in the name of Jesus, and commanded the spirit of blindness to depart. When I took my hand off her eye, she began to cry and shout, "I can see! I can see!"

I asked her to close her good eye and look at me with the previously blind eye. She affirmed that she could see me and everything else. I tested her further by asking her to count my raised fingers, and she counted them all. She could see with both eyes. A few days later, I received this testimony from her:

> "Thank you so much for the amazing services that you brought to New Day Christian Center in Follansbee, West Virginia! You gave me the miracle to see out of my left eye. I have been blind in that eye since birth!

Joseph Achanya

> You are an amazing man of God! Just keep spreading the gospel and doing Kingdom work! Hallelujah! Praise Jesus!"
>
> – Betty Burrier

I am a witness that Jesus is alive and that His miracles still happen today. A few months ago, we were in Laredo, Texas. A man who wasn't saved came to the service with his niece. He had been suffering from kidney stones for many years. When he heard my preaching on the first night, he got saved and was baptized in the Holy Ghost. On one of the nights, I prayed for him, and he left the service. A few weeks later, I got a message from his niece: "I invited my aunt and uncle to your services. Not only did they give their lives to Christ, but my uncle was due for surgery to remove kidney stones. He had been in pain for some days, and that day the Lord used you to heal him. He went back to the doctor, and the stone was gone. His surgery was canceled. Hallelujah, praise the Lord!"

Can you explain that? It is a miracle from God. One minute, the stone was there, and the next minute, it was not. It is a miracle that the blind can see again, the lame can walk again, and the kidney stone was no longer found. I am a witness that miracles still happen today.

These are testimonies of the blind seeing, the lame walking, incurable diseases being healed, and kidney stones disappearing—just like in Bible days. If you do not believe this, you don't believe the Bible. But here are a few witnesses to encourage you: if you believe in God for a miracle, He hasn't closed shop on miracles. Miracles are still happening today, and you can believe and expect a miracle from God.

Chapter Ten

Cessationism Debunked With Seven Questions

Cessationism is a belief in Christianity that originated during the Reformation. It states that gifts such as healing, prophecy, and tongues ceased at the end of the apostolic age. Initially focused on these three gifts, modern cessationists now maintain that all spiritual gifts ceased with the passing of the last apostles. This belief leads them to ridicule those who pray for healing today. Unfortunately, millions adhere to cessationist doctrine, with entire churches and traveling preachers dedicated to promoting this perspective. One might think that nobody believes in the cessationist gospel, but that is a misconception. Millions across Europe, America, and the rest of the world believe in it.

I believe that Christians should be able to defend what they believe. Most Christians, especially Pentecostals, cannot defend their beliefs. When asked about praying in tongues, many are at a loss for words. They struggle to explain scriptures, healing, speaking in tongues, or why Jesus is the only path to salvation. People find it challenging to articulate why the Bible, written over a thousand years ago, remains pertinent today and why living according to its teachings is essential.

We need to defend healings, tongues, and prophecy. We need to defend our faith. If an unbeliever mocks miracles, that is fine because they are unbelievers. However, the only way to defend miracles to an unbeliever is through miracles.

I am doing this in defense of miracles, tongues, and prophecy. If an unbeliever mocks miracles and passes snide comments, it does not move me at all. I cannot use the Bible to explain miracles to someone who does not believe in the Scriptures in the first place. However, if a Christian says they do not believe in miracles but believe in the Bible and in Jesus, that leaves me with many questions. I have highlighted seven questions from the Bible to ask.

The First Question – What about the Great Commission?

My first question is from the Great Commission:

> *And he said unto them, Go ye into all the world, and preach the gospel to every creature. He that believeth and is baptized shall be saved; but he that believeth not shall be damned. And these signs shall follow them that believe; In my name shall they cast out devils; they shall speak with new tongues; They shall take up serpents; and if they drink any deadly thing, it shall not hurt them; they shall lay hands on the sick, and they shall recover.*
>
> — Mark 16:15-18

Signs and Wonders Follow You

The scripture says that signs will follow anyone who believes, not just the apostles. He said, "You will cast out demons, speak with new tongues, be able to handle snakes with safety, and if you drink any poisonous thing, it will not hurt you. If you place your hand on the sick, they will recover." If you say miracles ended with the last apostle, what about this scripture? Why did Jesus give this command and command us to preach? If miracles ended with the apostolic age, my first question is: has the command to preach the gospel ended with the apostolic age?

Because they are all intertwined. Should we stop preaching the gospel to the lost? If you go down to verse 20, it says,

> *And they went forth, and preached every where, the*
>   *Lord working with them, and confirming the word*
>   *with signs following. Amen.*

So, the gifts of the Spirit are all confirmation of the gospel. Has God stopped confirming the preaching of the gospel? Or should we cease preaching the gospel? If the gifts of the Spirit have ceased today, how then would God confirm the gospel? Hebrews 2:4 says, "God also bearing them witness, both with signs and wonders, and with divers miracles, and gifts of the Holy Ghost, according to his own will." God never leaves the preaching of the gospel without confirmation.

The Second Question – Does the Emergence of False Prophets Not Confirm the Existence of True Prophets?

> *For in those days shall be affliction, such as was not*
>   *from the beginning of the creation which God*

> *created unto this time, neither shall be. And except that the Lord had shortened those days, no flesh should be saved: but for the elect's sake, whom he hath chosen, he hath shortened the days. And then if any man shall say to you, Lo, here is Christ; or, lo, he is there; believe him not: For false Christs and false prophets shall rise, and shall shew signs and wonders, to seduce, if it were possible, even the elect.*
>
> — Mark 13:19-22

Jesus was asked about the signs of the end times, and he mentioned the rise of false prophets in the last days. Other scriptures discuss this as well. My second question is: if the Bible talks about the rise of false prophets in the last days, is that not a sign that there will be good prophets in the last days? There cannot be false prophets without true prophets. There cannot be a counterfeit without an original. So, my question to those who say the gifts of the Spirit have passed away is: how about the rise of false prophets in the last days?

Look at the prophecy of Joel:

> *And it shall come to pass afterward, that I will pour out my spirit upon all flesh; and your sons and your daughters shall prophesy, your old men shall dream dreams, your young men shall see visions.*
>
> — Joel 2:28

If you say the gifts of prophecy, healing, and tongues have passed away, what do you say about this scripture? It says, 'In the last days...,' not 'the beginning of the last days.'

What time are we living in now? We are living in the last days. We are living in the last moments of the last days. I believe there will be more manifestations of that scripture today.

The Third Question – Is God a Respecter of Persons?

Jesus Christ the same yesterday, and to day, and for ever.

— Hebrews 13:8

Is God a respecter of persons? Does God have respect for the apostolic age but not for us? Wherever I go to preach, I usually say that there are three things that God has no respect for: years (times), people, and places. I can defend this from the Scripture.

God does not have more respect for the 80s than He has for the 60s or the 90s. God has no respect for people. The Bible says, "What I say to one, I say to all" (Mark 13:37). The Bible has no respect for places. God is not more in Jerusalem than He is in the United States or in Nigeria. God only respects faith. So, when you say the gift of the Spirit ended in the apostolic age, remember Acts 10, when the Gentile got baptized in the Holy Ghost. What was Peter's defense for it? He said, "This is a clear indication that God is not a respecter of persons" (Acts 10:34).

Jesus is the same yesterday, today, and forever. He has not lost His power. He only respects our faith. This is why the Bible says in the Great Commission, "Anyone who believes will cast out devils and raise the dead." So, the unifier is faith, which unifies every generation. If you say healing has passed away, then faith has also passed away. God is not a respecter of persons.

The Fourth Question – What Is Your Scriptural Defense for This Gospel?

This beginning of miracles did Jesus in Cana of Galilee,
   and manifested forth his glory; and his disciples
   believed on him.

— John 2:11

This is a scriptural defense of when miracles began. What is your scriptural defense of when miracles ended?

The Fifth Question – What Year Did the Apostolic Age Come to an End?

If you say miracles ended with the apostolic age, in what year did the apostolic age end? Was there a specific day when the last apostle died, and suddenly, no one could perform miracles anymore? My scripture to refute this is very simple. If you claim that miracles ceased with the last apostle, were only the apostles capable of performing miracles? Because upon reading through the epistles, you will find individuals other than the apostles who also performed miracles. The Bible mentions Stephen and Philip. Furthermore, the Bible discusses the brother of Philip:

And when we had finished our course from Tyre, we
   came to Ptolemais, and saluted the brethren, and
   abode with them one day. And the next day we that
   were of Paul's company departed, and came unto

> *Caesarea: and we entered into the house of Philip the evangelist, which was one of the seven; and abode with him. And the same man had four daughters, virgins, which did prophesy.*
>
> — Acts 21:7-9

It wasn't just the apostles who were performing miracles. Philip also had four daughters who could prophesy. If you say that the gift of prophecy no longer exists since the apostles died, the question is: Philip's daughters also prophesied. Agabus was also a prophet:

> *And as we tarried there many days, there came down from Judaea a certain prophet, named Agabus.*
>
> — Acts 21:10

So, Philip and Agabus prophesied, as did the daughters of Philip. When did the Spirit of prophecy cease? It has moved from one generation to another until today. While you are busy writing books about cessationism or creating podcasts and video clips about it, we have been traveling around the world proving that the Spirit of God still works wonders today. God still uses people today.

The Sixth Question – Do You Believe in the Rapture?

Cessationists tell people who are sick that they will be made whole in the rapture, referring to it as the "sweet by and by." My sixth question concerns the rapture. If you believe, as the Bible says in 1 Corinthians 15:51, that at the sound of the last trumpet, in the twinkling of an eye, the dead will be raised imperishable, and we will be changed, for the perishable must clothe itself with the imperishable and the mortal with immortality, how can you not believe that God can heal a headache, leg pain, tumor, cancer, or diabetes? If you believe in the rapture, then you believe in miracles.

The Seventh Question – Why Do You Believe That God Is No Longer Capable of Performing What Is Easier?

> *And, behold, they brought to him a man sick of the palsy, lying on a bed: and Jesus seeing their faith said unto the sick of the palsy; Son, be of good cheer; thy sins be forgiven thee. And, behold, certain of the scribes said within themselves, This man blasphemeth. And Jesus knowing their thoughts said, Wherefore think ye evil in your hearts? For whether is easier, to say, Thy sins be forgiven thee; or to say, Arise, and walk? But that ye may know that the Son of man hath power on earth to forgive sins, (then saith he to the sick of the palsy,) Arise, take up thy bed, and go unto thine house. And he arose, and departed to his house.*
>
> — Matthew 9:2-7

Jesus stood in front of a paralyzed man and declared that his sins were forgiven. This action angered the religious leaders, prompting Jesus to question them, "Which is easier? To say to the man, 'Rise up and walk,' or to say to him, 'Your sins are forgiven'?" Jesus was illustrating that instructing the man to rise and walk was the simpler task.

Signs and Wonders Follow You

My question to you is: Why do you believe that God is no longer capable of performing what is easier but can still accomplish what is more difficult? How is it that God seemingly cannot command someone to rise and walk, yet He can declare, "Your sins are forgiven"?

In this scripture, Jesus emphasized that instructing a sick individual to rise and walk was a simpler feat than declaring forgiveness of sins. You say that God does not heal anymore and that miracles have passed away, but Jesus said healing is easier. So, why do you think the easier has passed away and the difficult is still present today? The mistake people make regarding healing, and why they struggle with seeing miracles and operating in the Spirit's demonstration and power, is that they try to separate sin from sickness. Sickness came as a consequence of sin, so if sin has been forgiven, shouldn't the consequence be pardoned? Sin brought disease, pain, and suffering. If sin has been pardoned, then its consequences must be taken away.

I think religion does not have the power to solve people's problems and does not want to be put on the scene. If I say I believe in miracles and someone brings a sick person to me to pray for, and I cannot do anything about it, this is why people do not preach miracles. They preach against it because they are afraid of what will happen when they pray for people and they aren't healed.

In Matthew Chapter 17, a sick boy with epilepsy was brought to the apostles, but they could not cast out the demons. Then Jesus arrived and successfully cast out the demons. This raises the question: When the apostles prayed for the child and could not heal him, does that mean God doesn't heal today? No, it just means they could not do it. It does not negate the reality of miracles. If I pray for you and you do not get well, it simply means I couldn't do it. You can seek someone whom God would use to heal you.

After experiencing many failed attempts at healing, some people conclude that it is not God's will for them to be healed. That is far from the truth. God delights in seeing you well. It is not that it is not His will; it just means the person who prayed for you could not do it, and you can seek someone who can. Do not give up on your miracles.

Today, there is a need for notable miracles as seen in Acts 5, where it was proclaimed of the disciples, "A notable miracle has been done through them is evident to all who dwell in Jerusalem, and we cannot deny it." There is an urgent need for miracles that cannot be denied. People need to rise up and believe in undeniable miracles. If there are miracles that cannot be denied, then there would be no need for lengthy explanations. Notable miracles are what I believe God for everywhere I go to preach.

I shared a video some time ago of a lady who came to a program where I preached in West Virginia. She had three incurable diseases: a wound in her ear that the doctor said would never heal, hair loss due to cancer treatment, and a large abdominal hernia that displaced her spine. She returned to her workplace, and people saw her and could not believe it. This is the kind of miracle I am talking about—notable miracles. Another lady had a hole in her heart for sixty years.

She went back to the doctor, and there was no longer a hole in her heart. This is a miracle that cannot be denied, and that is why we must press in to see notable miracles. One miracle ends every argument. Some people claim healings are mental suggestions, saying we psych people to get well. Can I mentally psych lame legs to walk, blind eyes to see, or the dead to live? Without proof, we are in trouble, but with proof, the devil is in trouble. And we have proof. We have reports from doctors and testimonies from people. We have evidence of what we believe.

I remember the story of John Osteen, the father of Joel Osteen. He was a Baptist preacher who did not believe in miracles, tongues, or the gifts of the Spirit. One day, T.L. Osborn said to John, "Look, we do not have to argue. Come with me to one of my meetings and see the people who are testifying. Tell me if they are lying. Confirm the miracles yourself." John Osteen agreed and went to a meeting. T.L. Osborn preached, and John Osteen stood in front to confirm the miracles. He cried when he saw a lame person rise from a wheelchair and said, "This is real." He saw blind eyes opening and cried and cried. From that day, he became Pentecostal. We have proof for what we believe!

Chapter Eleven

Healing Scriptures

Surely he hath borne our griefs, and carried our sorrows: yet we did esteem him stricken, smitten of God, and afflicted. But he was wounded for our transgressions, he was bruised for our iniquities: the chastisement of our peace was upon him; and with his stripes we are healed.

— Isaiah 53:4-5

That it might be fulfilled which was spoken by Esaias the prophet, saying, Himself took our infirmities, and bare our sicknesses.

— Matthew 8:17

Who his own self bare our sins in his own body on the tree, that we, being dead to sins, should live unto righteousness: by whose stripes ye were healed.

— 1 Peter 2:24

*Bless the Lord, O my soul: and all that is within me,
bless his holy name. Bless the Lord, O my soul, and
forget not all his benefits: who forgiveth all thine
iniquities; who healeth all thy diseases; who
redeemeth thy life from destruction; who crowneth
thee with lovingkindness and tender mercies; who
satisfieth thy mouth with good things; so that thy
youth is renewed like the eagle's.*

— Psalm 103:1-5

*And said, If thou wilt diligently hearken to the voice of
the LORD thy God, and wilt do that which is right
in his sight, and wilt give ear to his commandments,
and keep all his statutes, I will put none of these
diseases upon thee, which I have brought upon the
Egyptians: for I am the LORD that healeth thee.*

— Exodus 15:26

*And the LORD will take away from thee all sickness,
and will put none of the evil diseases of Egypt,
which thou knowest, upon thee; but will lay them
upon all them that hate thee.*

— Deuteronomy 7:15

*For I will restore health unto thee, and I will heal thee
of thy wounds, saith the LORD.*

— Jeremiah 30:17

Behold, I will bring it health and cure, and I will cure

them, and will reveal unto them the abundance of peace and truth.

— Jeremiah 33:6

Beloved, I wish above all things that thou mayest prosper and be in health, even as thy soul prospereth.

— 3 John 1:2

He that spared not his own Son, but delivered him up for us all, how shall he not with him also freely give us all things?

— Romans 8:32

Every good gift and every perfect gift is from above, and cometh down from the Father of lights, with whom is no variableness, neither shadow of turning.

— James 1:17

Then shall thy light break forth as the morning, and thine health shall spring forth speedily: and thy righteousness shall go before thee; the glory of the LORD shall be thy reward.

— Isaiah 58:8

Turn again, and tell Hezekiah the captain of my people, Thus saith the LORD, the God of David thy father, I have heard thy prayer, I have seen thy tears: behold, I will heal thee.

— 2 Kings 20:5

God is not a man, that he should lie; neither the son of man, that he should repent: hath he said, and shall he not do it? or hath he spoken, and shall he not make it good?

— Numbers 23:19

He brought them forth also with silver and gold: and there was not one feeble person among their tribes.

— Psalms 105:37

He healeth the broken in heart, and bindeth up their wounds.

— Psalms 147:3

O LORD my God, I cried unto thee, and thou hast healed me.

— Psalms 30:2

Many are the afflictions of the righteous: but the LORD delivereth him out of them all.

— Psalms 34:19

If ye then, being evil, know how to give good gifts unto your children, how much more shall your Father

*which is in heaven give good things to them that
ask him?*

— Matthew 7:11

*Christ hath redeemed us from the curse of the law,
being made a curse for us: for it is written, Cursed
is every one that hangeth on a tree. That the
blessing of Abraham might come on the Gentiles
through Jesus Christ; that we might receive the
promise of the Spirit through faith. And if ye be
Christ's, then are ye Abraham's seed, and heirs
according to the promise.*

— Galatians 3:13, 14, 29

*Giving thanks unto the Father, which hath made us
meet to be partakers of the inheritance of the saints
in light: Who hath delivered us from the power of
darkness, and hath translated us into the kingdom
of his dear Son: In whom we have redemption
through his blood, even the forgiveness of sins.*

— Colossians 1:12-14

*And ye are complete in him, which is the head of all
principality and power: And having spoiled principalities and powers, he made a show of them
openly, triumphing over them in it.*

— Colossians 2:10, 15

*And the very God of peace sanctify you wholly; and I
pray God your whole spirit and soul and body be*

preserved blameless unto the coming of our Lord Jesus Christ.

— 1 Thessalonians 5:23

Ye shall walk in all the ways which the LORD your God hath commanded you, that ye may live, and that it may be well with you, and that ye may prolong your days in the land which ye shall possess.

— Deuteronomy 5:33

My son, forget not my law; but let thine heart keep my commandments: For length of days, and long life, and peace, shall they add to thee.

— Proverbs 3:1-2

For by me thy days shall be multiplied, and the years of thy life shall be increased.

— Proverbs 9:11

But they that wait upon the LORD shall renew their strength; they shall mount up with wings as eagles; they shall run, and not be weary; and they shall walk, and not faint.

— Isaiah 40:31

They shall not build, and another inhabit; they shall not plant, and another eat: for as the days of a tree

*are the days of my people, and mine elect shall long
enjoy the work of their hands.*

— Isaiah 65:22

*And Jesus went about all Galilee, teaching in their
synagogues, and preaching the gospel of the kingdom, and healing all manner of sickness and all
manner of disease among the people. And his fame
went throughout all Syria: and they brought unto
him all sick people that were taken with divers
diseases and torments, and those which were
possessed with devils, and those which were lunatic,
and those that had the palsy; and he healed them.*

— Matthew 4:23-24

*And, behold, there came a leper and worshipped him,
saying, Lord, if thou wilt, thou canst make me
clean. And Jesus put forth his hand, and touched
him, saying, I will; be thou clean. And immediately
his leprosy was cleansed.*

— Matthew 8:2-3

*The thief cometh not, but for to steal, and to kill, and
to destroy: I am come that they might have life, and
that they might have it more abundantly.*

— John 10:10

*How God anointed Jesus of Nazareth with the Holy
Ghost and with power: who went about doing*

good, and healing all that were oppressed of the devil; for God was with him.

— Acts 10:38

Jesus Christ the same yesterday, and today, and for ever.

— Hebrews 13:8

For this purpose the Son of God was manifested, that he might destroy the works of the devil.

— 1 John 3:8

Come unto me, all ye that labour and are heavy laden, and I will give you rest. Take my yoke upon you, and learn of me; for I am meek and lowly in heart: and ye shall find rest unto your souls. For my yoke is easy, and my burden is light.

— Matthew 11:28-30

But when Jesus knew it, he withdrew himself from thence: and great multitudes followed him, and he healed them all.

— Matthew 12:15

When Jesus heard of it, he departed thence by ship into a desert place apart: and when the people had heard thereof, they followed him on foot out of the cities. And Jesus went forth, and saw a great multi-

*tude, and was moved with compassion toward
them, and he healed their sick.*

— Matthew 14:13-14

*And when they were gone over, they came into the land
of Gennesaret. And when the men of that place had
knowledge of him, they sent out into all that
country round about, and brought unto him all
that were diseased; And besought him that they
might only touch the hem of his garment: and as
many as touched were made perfectly whole.*

— Matthew 14:34-36

*And Jesus departed from thence, and came nigh unto
the sea of Galilee; and went up into a mountain,
and sat down there. And great multitudes came
unto him, having with them those that were lame,
blind, dumb, maimed, and many others, and cast
them down at Jesus' feet; and he healed them: Insomuch that the multitude wondered, when they saw
the dumb to speak, the maimed to be whole, the
lame to walk, and the blind to see: and they glorified the God of Israel.*

— Matthew 15:29-31

*And he arose out of the synagogue, and entered into
Simon's house. And Simon's wife's mother was
taken with a great fever; and they besought him for
her. And he stood over her, and rebuked the fever;
and it left her: and immediately she arose and
ministered unto them.*

— Luke 4:38-39

*Now when the sun was setting, all they that had any
sick with divers diseases brought them unto him;
and he laid his hands on every one of them, and
healed them. And devils also came out of many,
crying out, and saying, Thou art Christ the Son of
God. And he rebuking them suffered them not to
speak: for they knew that he was Christ.*

— Luke 4:40-41

*And when he had called unto him his twelve disciples,
he gave them power against unclean spirits, to cast
them out, and to heal all manner of sickness and all
manner of disease.*

— Matthew 10:1

*And he said unto them, Go ye into all the world, and
preach the gospel to every creature. He that
believeth and is baptized shall be saved; but he that
believeth not shall be damned. And these signs
shall follow them that believe; In my name shall
they cast out devils; they shall speak with new
tongues; They shall take up serpents; and if they
drink any deadly thing, it shall not hurt them; they*

shall lay hands on the sick, and they shall recover. So then after the Lord had spoken unto them, he was received up into heaven, and sat on the right hand of God. And they went forth, and preached every where, the Lord working with them, and confirming the word with signs following. Amen.

— Mark 16:15-20

Verily, verily, I say unto you, He that believeth on me, the works that I do shall he do also; and greater works than these shall he do; because I go unto my Father. And whatsoever ye shall ask in my name, that will I do, that the Father may be glorified in the Son. If ye shall ask any thing in my name, I will do it. If ye love me, keep my commandments.

— John 14:12-15

And the people with one accord gave heed unto those things which Philip spake, hearing and seeing the miracles which he did. For unclean spirits, crying with loud voice, came out of many that were possessed with them: and many taken with palsies, and that were lame, were healed.

— Acts 8:6-7

*And there he found a certain man named Aeneas,
which had kept his bed eight years, and was sick of
the palsy. And Peter said unto him, Aeneas, Jesus
Christ maketh thee whole: arise, and make thy bed.
And he arose immediately. And all that dwelt at
Lydda and Saron saw him, and turned to the Lord.*

— Acts 9:33-35

*And there sat a certain man at Lystra, impotent in his
feet, being a cripple from his mother's womb, who
never had walked: The same heard Paul speak: who
stedfastly beholding him, and perceiving that he
had faith to be healed, Said with a loud voice,
Stand upright on thy feet. And he leaped and
walked.*

— Acts 14:8-10

*And God wrought special miracles by the hands of
Paul: So that from his body were brought unto the
sick handkerchiefs or aprons, and the diseases
departed from them, and the evil spirits went out of
them.*

— Acts 19:11-12

*Is any sick among you? let him call for the elders of the
church; and let them pray over him, anointing him
with oil in the name of the Lord: And the prayer of
faith shall save the sick, and the Lord shall raise
him up; and if he have committed sins, they shall be
forgiven him. Confess your faults one to another,
and pray one for another, that ye may be healed.*

The effectual fervent prayer of a righteous man availeth much.

— James 5:14-16

But unto you that fear my name shall the Sun of righteousness arise with healing in his wings; and ye shall go forth, and grow up as calves of the stall.

— Malachi 4:2

And being found in fashion as a man, he humbled himself, and became obedient unto death, even the death of the cross. Wherefore God also hath highly exalted him, and given him a name which is above every name: That at the name of Jesus every knee should bow, of things in heaven, and things in earth, and things under the earth.

— Philippians 2:8-10

And in that day ye shall ask me nothing. Verily, verily, I say unto you, Whatsoever ye shall ask the Father in my name, he will give it you. Hitherto have ye asked nothing in my name: ask, and ye shall receive, that your joy may be full.

— John 16:23-24

And whatsoever ye shall ask in my name, that will I do, that the Father may be glorified in the Son. If ye shall ask any thing in my name, I will do it.

— John 14:13-14

Joseph Achanya

> *Again I say unto you, That if two of you shall agree on earth as touching any thing that they shall ask, it shall be done for them of my Father which is in heaven.*
>
> — Matthew 18:19

> *(As it is written, I have made thee a father of many nations,) before him whom he believed, even God, who quickeneth the dead, and calleth those things which be not as though they were. And being not weak in faith, he considered not his own body now dead, when he was about an hundred years old, neither yet the deadness of Sarah's womb: He staggered not at the promise of God through unbelief; but was strong in faith, giving glory to God; And being fully persuaded that, what he had promised, he was able also to perform.*
>
> — Romans 4:17, 19-21

> *So then faith cometh by hearing, and hearing by the word of God.*
>
> — Romans 10:17

> *Know ye not that ye are the temple of God, and that the Spirit of God dwelleth in you?*
>
> — 1 Corinthians 3:16

Signs and Wonders Follow You

For the law of the Spirit of life in Christ Jesus hath made me free from the law of sin and death.

— Romans 8:2

Ye are of God, little children, and have overcome them: because greater is he that is in you, than he that is in the world.

— 1 John 4:4

But if the Spirit of him that raised up Jesus from the dead dwell in you, he that raised up Christ from the dead shall also quicken your mortal bodies by his Spirit that dwelleth in you.

— Romans 8:11

Forasmuch then as the children are partakers of flesh and blood, he also himself likewise took part of the same; that through death he might destroy him that had the power of death, that is, the devil; And deliver them who through fear of death were all their lifetime subject to bondage.

— Hebrews 2:14-15

When the even was come, they brought unto him many that were possessed with devils: and he cast out the spirits with his word, and healed all that were sick.

— Matthew 8:16

If ye abide in me, and my words abide in you, ye shall ask what ye will, and it shall be done unto you.

— John 15:7

He sent his word, and healed them, and delivered them from their destructions.

— Psalms 107:20

And they overcame him by the blood of the Lamb, and by the word of their testimony; and they loved not their lives unto the death.

— Revelations 12:11

Let the weak say, I am strong.

— Joel 3:10

I call heaven and earth to record this day against you, that I have set before you life and death, blessing and cursing: therefore choose life, that both thou and thy seed may live: That thou mayest love the Lord thy God, and that thou mayest obey his voice, and that thou mayest cleave unto him: for he is thy life, and the length of thy days: that thou mayest dwell in the land which the Lord sware unto thy fathers, to Abraham, to Isaac, and to Jacob, to give them.

— Deuteronomy 30:19-20

Signs and Wonders Follow You

I shall not die, but live, and declare the works of the Lord.

— Psalm 118:17

Fear thou not; for I am with thee: be not dismayed; for I am thy God: I will strengthen thee; yea, I will help thee; yea, I will uphold thee with the right hand of my righteousness.

— Isaiah 41:10

Then said the Lord unto me, Thou hast well seen: for I will hasten my word to perform it.

— Jeremiah 1:12

Heal me, O Lord, and I shall be healed; save me, and I shall be saved: for thou art my praise.

— Jeremiah 17:14

What do ye imagine against the Lord? he will make an utter end: affliction shall not rise up the second time.

— Nahum 1:9

Jesus said unto him, If thou canst believe, all things are possible to him that believeth.

— Mark 9:23

And Jesus looking upon them saith, With men it is

> *impossible, but not with God: for with God all things are possible.*
>
> — Mark 10:27

> *And Jesus answering saith unto them, Have faith in God. For verily I say unto you, That whosoever shall say unto this mountain, Be thou removed, and be thou cast into the sea; and shall not doubt in his heart, but shall believe that those things which he saith shall come to pass; he shall have whatsoever he saith. Therefore I say unto you, What things soever ye desire, when ye pray, believe that ye receive them, and ye shall have them.*
>
> — Mark 11:22-24

Chapter Twelve

Healing Prayer

I want to lead you in a prayer to receive Jesus into your heart. When He comes in, your sickness is in trouble. When He comes in, your disease is in trouble. When He comes in, your trouble is in trouble. The Bible says that light shines in darkness, and darkness does not comprehend it. Receive the Lord Jesus. When you make the Lord Jesus the Lord of your life, you become a lord over principalities and powers. You become a lord over sicknesses and diseases. You become a lord over pain and suffering.

I am going to lead you in a prayer of confession right where you are. Repeat this prayer aloud. The Bible says that if you believe in your heart and confess with your mouth the Lord Jesus, you will be saved. What will you be saved from? You will be saved from your sins and the consequences thereof. You will be saved from your sicknesses, diseases, and pains. Salvation is an all-inclusive word. Choose this day whom you will serve. Choose Jesus as your master. We will pray a prayer of salvation now and of healing later. If you believe, rejoice first and thank Him in your own words. These words are not empty words. God hears every word, and He draws near to you right now. As He draws near to you, your sickness and diseases are shaking because they have to go.

Say these words:

> "Oh, Lord God, I call on your name, Jesus. I repent of my sins. Forgive me today and take away my past. I believe You died for me and I accept the gospel. I believe Jesus is the Son of God who died on the cross for me and shed His blood for my sins. Thank You for loving me. In this moment, I give You my life and accept You as my Savior. I receive life through Jesus Christ and welcome You into my heart. Right now, I am forgiven, my sins are gone, I am changed, and I am a child of God. My life is new. Thank You, Jesus! You live in me now. Satan, you are no longer my master; Jesus is my Lord and Savior, and I have His peace and His joy. Amen. Hallelujah!"

Take a few minutes and thank Him in your own words because He lives in you now and all of your sins are gone and they are nowhere to be found. Say this with me right now:

> "Oh, Lord, heal me as You have saved me. Jesus, I receive Your healing. You are my Healer, and You are healing me. The sickness I had was caused by the spirit of infirmity, but it has been destroyed and has left me. I am healed, and the life of my sickness is gone. My sickness is dead. I believe that I am whole. Hallelujah! Right now, I am healed, made new, and my body is the temple of the Holy Ghost, not the house of

disease. Glory to God! I am free from pain and disease. Hallelujah!"

Now, clap your hands and thank Him. Rejoice and be glad about it. Act like you believe. Put your faith in action and expect a miracle from God. Your faith has made you well in Jesus' Name. Amen.

Shaking Your Generation
The Believer's Call to Global Impact

Introduction

As thou hast sent me into the world, even so have I also sent them into the world.

— John 17:18

Jesus, during His 33 years of life, focused solely on ministry for only three and a half years. However, the global impact He made in those three years cannot be denied; He shook the world.

The Apostles, taking over after Jesus, continued with the same intensity, shaking their generation. It was even said that they turned the world upside down (Acts 17:86). Now, it is our turn. In our hands rests the sacred baton passed down through the ages. Jesus expects us to carry forward the mission and maintain the same intensity of impact.

In this book, I unveil the secret recipe that Jesus and the Apostles utilized to shake their world, leaving an enduring legacy that resonates to this day. Why should we seek to substitute an already proven method? The value of this book lies in its ability to reveal the pattern needed to impact and transform your generation, allowing you to fulfill your mission. It serves as a radiant torch, guiding millions of believers, gospel workers, Bible students, preachers, and ministers, and enabling them to become global Apostles, Evangelists, Pastors, Prophets, and Teachers. You possess everything necessary to shake your generation. Read this book and leave an indelible impact on your world.

* * *

Available in Paperback and eBook from Your Favorite Bookstore or Online Retailer

About the Author

Evangelist Joseph Achanya is the founder of Mega Harvest and the host of the "Heal the Sick" radio and TV broadcast. Evangelist Achanya passionately makes Jesus known to today's generation. He has led many international open-air crusades and outreaches under the theme "THIS SAME JESUS," demonstrating the power of the resurrected Christ through signs, wonders, and miracles. Inspired by the ministry of Dr. T.L. Osborn, Evangelist Achanya dedicates his ministry to winning the lost and showcasing the transformative power of Christ. He is a sought-after preacher whose renowned miracle ministry is changing thousands of lives worldwide.

MegaHarvest.org

facebook.com/preacherjay
x.com/preacher_jay
instagram.com/preacher_jay
youtube.com/PreacherJay

www.ingramcontent.com/pod-product-compliance
Lightning Source LLC
LaVergne TN
LVHW041230080426
835508LV00011B/1131